Country Music
~ Says It All ~

Lyrics of Livin',
Lovin', and Leavin'

Compiled by
Betty Blair Daniel, Emmie Thomas, and Jim Thomas

LONGSTREET PRESS, IN
Atlanta, Georgia

D1059087

Published by LONGSTREET PRESS, INC.,
a subsidiary of Cox Newspapers,
a division of Cox Enterprises, Inc.
2140 Newmarket Parkway
Suite 118
Marietta, Georgia 30067

Printed in the United States of America

1st printing, 1995

Library of Congress Catalog Number: 94-74230

ISBN: 1-56352-213-6

This book was printed by Quebecor / Kingsport, TN

Film Preparation by Holland Graphics, Inc., Mableton, GA

Cover design by Tonya Beach
Book design by Jill Dible

Foreword

Everyone who has ever listened to the radio knows exactly what is meant by the expression, "I can't get that song out of my head." Hopefully for better, sometimes for worse, a songwriter "hooks" us with a line or verse that our mind replays over and over. Often the song is some mindless ditty conceived to have just such an intrusive effect, but sometimes we're blessed with the words of a voice that is speaking to us, about our lives, capturing the essence of a part of life so purely that it seems as though the song could have been written about us, and for us.

Perhaps more consistently and clearly than any other form of popular music, country songs capture the sentiments and stories of everyday life. So it is not surprising that once again country music is experiencing a boom in popularity as more people discover a form of music that simply and eloquently speaks to them about life on life's terms. Arguably, nowhere in the music business are great songs and songwriters more important than in country music.

The following pages are in recognition of the immensely talented, but often obscure men and women who fuel the fires of country music. While far from a complete list, we think it's a good start. Our hope is, that by reducing the songs to lyrical excerpts without melody or voice, we can begin to distinguish between poetry and popularity.

We would also hope that the reading of this book will have the same effect on you that the research had on us; pulling out old records from home, looking for recordings at the store, and requesting songs on the radio.

And when the songs you've heard play over and over in your mind, you'll know that the songwriter has you "hooked."

Note: *Throughout the book, many songs have a ranking based on* Billboard *magazine's annual chart. For example, a #52 song of the year typically would reflect #1 chart status for one of the year's 52 weeks. Prior to the publication of* Billboard, *rankings were derived from record sales. Starred songs denote the best lyrics, based on our judgment of the star appeal of the recording artist.*

Cover Art
by the Reverend Howard Finster, Summerville, Georgia

About the artist:

Many years ago, near the end of his church service, the Reverend Howard Finster asked his congregation what they remembered from the sermon he had just completed.

On learning that not a soul in the congregation could recall the sermon's message, Finster gave up preaching and started doing odd jobs and repairs.

In 1976, he gave up his repair businesses when he had a vision in which God commanded him to become an artist and create sacred folk art.

Over his nearly twenty-year career as an artist, Finster has created over 35,000 works of art. His paintings have been used in the cover art of albums by R.E.M. and the Talking Heads. The cover of this book features an interpretation of Hank Williams, Sr.

During his career, Finster has transformed what used to be his home into "Paradise Garden," a folk art environment that encompasses an incredible maze of mirrored sidewalks, sculptures, paintings and The World Folk Art Church. Underlying all his creative endeavors is Finster's mission to spread the word of God.

A poet as well as a visual artist, Finster inscribed the following verse on the back of the cover art:

"All along life's road
it's great to have a place of abode—
in hot weather or winter snow.
As for me I go and go.
I work from my head to my bottom toe."

Acknowledgments

We would like to express our thanks to these people who helped make this book possible:

Dave Weiner for the inspiration, Marge McDonald for the guidance, Gib Carson for the opportunity.

Clarence Selman and Bob Kirch for helping to get us started.

Ronnie Pugh and The Country Music Foundation for the use of their wonderful library.

We'd also like to thank the following people who are involved in licensing the use of song lyrics for their invaluable cooperation: Faye Smith at Broadcast Music Inc.; Jay Morgenstern, Jack Rozner and Marcia Costa at Warner-Chappell, Los Angeles; Johnny Wright at Warner-Chappell, Nashville; Suzanne Prokasy at Opryland Music; Claire Johnston at Peer Music; Kate Scott-Douglas at MCA; Rosemarie Gawelko at CPP Belwin; Katie Schweitzer at BMG; Teresa Robinson at Tom Collins Music; Eden Alpert at Rondor Music; Joan Schulman at Polygram; Beth Peters at Copyright Management; and Teddy Wilburn at Sure-Fire Music.

Thanks as well to Monty Powell, John Paul Daniel and Fred Daniel; and for giving this book its cover, sincere thanks to Howard Finster.

And last on the list but always first in our hearts, thanks to Momma.

Contents

Uncommon Sense

*W*e're all polyester poets and pickers of a kind,
With far too many questions
For the answers in our minds,
Stranded in the middle
Of all that's black and white,
Somewhere between ragged and right.

"Somewhere Between Ragged and Right"
Written by Waylon Jennings and Roger Murrah
Recorded by John Anderson

Mary Chapin Carpenter

*S*ometimes you're the windshield,
Sometimes you're the bug,
Sometimes it all comes together, baby,
Sometimes you're a fool in love.

Sometimes you're the Louisville Slugger,
Sometimes you're the ball,
Sometimes it all comes together, baby,
Sometimes you're gonna lose it all.

"The Bug"
Written by Mark Knopfler
Recorded by Mary Chapin Carpenter

Originally released in 1991 on Dire Strait's *On Every Street*.
This song became a country hit on
Mary Chapin Carpenter's 1992 album *Come On, Come On*.

Tom T. Hall

*A*in't but three things in this world
That's worth a solitary dime,
But old dogs, children and watermelon wine.

"Old Dogs, Children and Watermelon Wine"
Written by Tom T. Hall
Recorded by Tom T. Hall

#15 Song of Year in 1973

*W*hen you're downhearted
And when you're feeling blue,
Keep your chin up, keep your faith,
And keep this point of view —
Don't forget smiles are made out of sunshine,
And a smile goes a long, long way.

"Smiles Are Made Out Of Sunshine"
Written by Ray Gilbert
Recorded by Roy Rogers

Roy Rogers used this as his theme song.

*Y*ou can break your eggs
To count your chickens,
And you can break your neck
To keep your ducks in a row,
But don't think every chance you take
Has to mean a new mistake;
It ain't necessarily so.

Willie Nelson

"Ain't Necessarily So"
Written by Beth Nielson Chapman
Recorded by Willie Nelson

You've got to stand for something,
Or you'll fall for anything;
You've got to be your own man,
Not a puppet on a string.
Never compromise what's right
And uphold your family name;
You've got to stand for something,
Or you'll fall for anything.

"You've Got to Stand for Something"
Written by Aaron Tippin and Buddy Brock
Recorded by Aaron Tippin

7

I ain't got a dime, but what I got is mine;
I ain't rich, but Lord I'm free.
Amarillo by morning,
Amarillo is where I'll be.

"Amarillo by Morning"
Written by Terry Stafford and P. Frazer
Recorded by George Strait

Johnny Cash

*B*ad news travels like wildfire,
Good news travels slow.

"Bad News"
Written by John D. Loudermilk
Recorded by Johnny Cash

Harmony, harmony,
It touches something
Down at your very core;
There's something about
The sound of voices in accord,
Singing harmony.

"Harmony"
Written by Rick Beresford and Jimbo Hinson
Recorded by John Conlee

Kris Kristofferson

I'll never know till it's over
If I'm right or I'm wrong loving you,
But I'd rather be sorry for something I've done
Than for something that I didn't do.

"I'd Rather Be Sorry"
Written by Kris Kristofferson
Recorded by Ray Price

#16 Song of the Year in 1971

Let go, baby,
Let the wind blow through you hair.
You can't walk around in chains,
And ever get nowhere.
Something or someone
Is telling you it's over and done.
Outside the free wind blows,
Let go.

"Let Go"
Written by Dickie Brown
Recorded by Brother Phelps

Kathy Mattea

$\mathcal{T}$ime passes by, people pass on,
At the drop of a tear, they're gone.
Let's do what we dare, do what we like,
And love while we're here
Before time passes by.

"Time Passes By"
Written by Jon Vezner and Susan Longacre
Recorded by Kathy Mattea

Waylon Jennings

I've always been crazy,
But it's kept me from going insane;
Nobody knows if it's something to bless
   or to blame.
So far I ain't found the rhyme
   or a reason to change;
I've always been crazy,
But it keeps me from going insane.

"I've Always Been Crazy"
Written by Waylon Jennings
Recorded by Waylon Jennings

#4 Song of the Year in 1978

Two Timin'

Tammy Wynette

*W*e're just a pair of old sneakers,
We know that cheatin' is wrong.
We're just a pair of old sneakers,
And we've been in the closet too long.

"A Pair of Old Sneakers"
Written by Larry Kingston and Glenn Sutton
Recorded by George Jones and Tammy Wynette

Hank Williams, Sr.

*Y*our cheatin' heart will pine someday,
And crave the love you threw away;
The time will come when you'll be blue,
Your cheatin' heart will tell on you.

"Your Cheatin' Heart"
Written by Hank Williams, Sr.
Recorded by Hank Williams, Sr.

#2 Song of the Year in 1953

17

Doug Stone

*I'*d be better off in a pine box
On a slow train back to Georgia,
Or in the grey walls of a prison doin' time.
I think I'd rather die and go to hell
And face the Devil,
Than to lie here with you and him
Together on my mind.

"I'd Be Better Off in a Pine Box"
Written by Johnny MacRae and Steve Clark
Recorded by Doug Stone

#34 Song of the Year in 1990

Kitty Wells

It wasn't God who made honky-tonk angels,
As you said in the words of your song;
Too many times married men think
   they're still single,
   That has caused many a good girl
   to go wrong.

"It Wasn't God Who Made Honky-Tonk Angels"
Written by J. D. Miller
Recorded by Kitty Wells

#4 Song of the Year in 1952 for Kitty Wells, one of country's early female recording stars.
This song was Kitty's first big hit.

Loretta Lynn

*W*omen like you, they're a dime a dozen,
You can buy 'em anywhere.
For you to get to him, I'd have to move over,
And I'm gonna stand right here.
It'll be over my dead body, so get out
while you can,
Oh, you ain't woman enough to take my man.

"You Ain't Woman Enough"
Written by Loretta Lynn
Recorded by Loretta Lynn

#4 Song of the Year in 1966

True Love

Listen to the rain fallin' on the roof;
The thunder sounds like horses' hooves,
And I listen to her breathe,
   and it makes me want
To wake her up, and tell her I'm on fire
With morning desire

Kenny Rogers

"Morning Desire"
Written by Dave Loggins
Recorded by Kenny Rogers

#6 Song of the Year in 1986

*Y*ou are my sunshine, my only sunshine;
You make me happy when skies are gray;
You'll never know, dear, how much I love you;
Please don't take my sunshine away.

"You Are My Sunshine"
Written by Jimmie Davis
Recorded by Jimmie Davis

Jimmie Davis was elected governor of Louisiana in 1944. While in office he acted in two movies, one of which was *Take Me Back to Oklahoma* featuring the song "You Are My Sunshine" and starring Tex Ritter. The idea for "You Are My Sunshine" came to Jimmie on a fishing trip.

It takes a little rain
To make love grow;
It's the heartache and the pain
That makes the real heart show.
Where the sun always shines,
There's a desert below;
It takes a little rain to make love grow.

"It Takes a Little Rain"
Written by James Dean Hicks, Roger Murrah, and Steve Dean
Recorded by The Oak Ridge Boys

#10 Song of the Year in 1987

Tom T. Hall

I love honest open smiles,
Kisses from a child,
Tomatoes on a vine,
And onions.
I love winners when they cry,
Losers when they try,
Music when it's good,
And life.
And I love you, too.

"I Love"
Written by Tom T. Hall
Recorded by Tom T. Hall

#3 Song of the Year in 1974. Tom T. Hall has written every song he has recorded.

25

Tonight I saw a red, red rose in the yellow moon,
Shinin' on a silhouette,
Lyin' in the shadows of my bedroom.
I knew it when we made love,
And I couldn't quit calling her name,
That I'd been hit by another
Fast movin' train.

"Fast Movin' Train"
Written by Dave Loggins
Recorded by Restless Heart

#37 Song of the Year in 1990

I would count the steps from here to heaven,
And every heartache I was given,
Tip my hat and walk through fire,
To find sure love.

"Sure Love"
Written by Hal Ketchum and Gary Burr
Recorded by Hal Ketchum

Suzy Boguss

Blow you ol' blue northern,
    blow my love to me,
He's ridin' in tonight from California;
He loves his damned old rodeo
    as much as he loves me.
Someday soon,
Goin' with him,
Someday soon.

"Someday Soon"
Written by Ian Tyson
Originally recorded by Judy Collins, "Someday Soon"
was later a country hit for Suzy Boguss.

Ronnie Milsap

*K*iss me each morning for a million years,
Hold me each evening by your side;
Tell me you love me for a million years,
Then if it don't work out,
Then if it don't work out,
Then you can tell me goodbye.

"Then You Can Tell Me Goodbye"
Written by John D. Loudermilk
Recorded by Ronnie Milsap

Wynonna

*O*nly love sails straight from the harbor,
Only love will lead us to the other shore.
Out of all the flags I've flown,
One flies high and stands alone,
Only love.

"Only Love"
Written by Marcus Hummon and Roger Murrah
Recorded by Wynonna

#31 Song of the Year in 1993

Kathy Mattea

*W*hy don't we get caught in this moment,
Be victims of sweet circumstance.
Tonight I feel like all creation
Is asking us to dance.

"Asking Us to Dance"
Written by Hugh Prestwood
Recorded by Kathy Mattea

I've been throwing horseshoes
Over my left shoulder;
I've spent most of my life
Searching for that four-leaf clover.
Yet you run with me, chasing my rainbows —
Honey, I love you too;
That's the way love goes.

Merle Haggard

"That's the Way Love Goes"
Written by Sanger Shafer and Lefty Frizzell
Originally recorded by Johnny Rodriguez, later recorded by Merle Haggard.

#25 Song of the Year in 1974 for Johnny Rodriquez
#37 Song of the Year in 1984 for Merle Haggard. Merle won the Grammy for best male
country vocal with his recording of this song.

Like two sparrows in a hurricane
Trying to find their way,
With a head full of dreams
And faith that can move anything,
They've heard it's all uphill;
But all they know is how they feel.
The world says they'll never make it,
Love says they will.

"Two Sparrows in a Hurricane"
Written by Mark Alan Springer
Recorded by Tanya Tucker

*Y*ou see without love a house ain't a home,
A diamond ain't no more than a stone in the ground.
I'd give all the material things I own in this life,
If I could just hear the sound
Of a heartbeat in the darkness
Every night of my life.

"Heartbeat in the Darkness"
Written by Dave Loggins and Russell Smith
Recorded by Don Williams

#41 Song of the Year in 1986

Did you ever know that you are my hero
And everything I would like to be.
I can fly higher than an eagle;
You are the wind beneath my wings.

"The Wind Beneath My Wings"
Written by Larry Henley and Jeff Silbar
Recorded by Gary Morris

Gary Morris won the 1984 CMA Award for "Song of the Year" with his recording of this song.

Faded Love

I miss you, darling,
More and more everyday,
As heaven would miss the stars above;
With every heartbeat,
I still think of you
And remember our faded love.

"Faded Love"
Written by Bob Wills and John Wills
Originally recorded by Bob Wills, and later recorded by Patsy Cline.

#31 Song of the Year in 1963 for Patsy Cline

You told me just as plain as it could be,
How you needed to hear some words of love from me.
I never thought it mattered much,
Now it sure looks like it did.
Oh, why didn't I say the things
I should have said.

"Things I Should Have Said"
Written by John Paul Daniel and Shawna Harrington-Burkhart
Recorded by Clay Walker

I was waltzing with my darlin'
To the Tennessee Waltz,
When an old friend I happened to see;
Introduced him to my loved one,
And while they were waltzing,
My friend stole my sweetheart from me.

"Tennessee Waltz"
Written by Redd Stewart and Pee Wee King
Recorded by Pee Wee King, Cowboy Copas and also Roy Acuff

#11 Song of the Year in 1948 for Pee Wee King on RCA. #14 Song of the Year in 1948 for Cowboy Copas on King records. "Tennessee Waltz" was later voted the official Tennessee state song by the state legislature.

Vince Gill

The lonely sound of my voice calling
Is driving me insane.
Just like rain my tears keep falling;
Nobody answers when I call your name.

"When I Call Your Name"
Written by Vince Gill and Tim DuBois
Recorded by Vince Gill

Vince Gill won the 1991 Grammy for Best Male Country Vocal with his recording of this song. "When I Call Your Name" went on to win the 1991 CMA Awards for "Song of the Year" and "Single of the Year."

George Strait

*A*ll my ex's live in Texas,
And Texas is a place I'd dearly love to be;
But all my ex's live in Texas,
And that's why I hang my hat in Tennessee.

"All My Ex's Live in Texas"
Written by Sanger D. Shafer and Lyndia J. Shafer
Recorded by George Strait

A memory from your lonesome past
Keeps us so far apart;
Why can't I free your doubtful mind
And melt your cold, cold heart?

"Cold, Cold Heart"
Written by Hank Williams, Sr.
Recorded by Hank Williams, Sr.

#1 Song of the Year in 1951

If heartaches brought fame
In love's crazy game,
I'd be a legend in my time.

"A Legend in My Time"
Written by Don Gibson
Recorded by Don Gibson

Bill Monroe

It was on one moonlight night,
Stars shinin' bright,
Whisper on high,
Love said goodbye;
Blue moon of Kentucky keep on shining,
Shine on the one that's gone and left me blue.

"Blue Moon of Kentucky"
Written by Bill Monroe
Originally recorded by Bill Monroe and later recorded by Elvis Presley.

"Blue Moon of Kentucky" was the B-side to Elvis Presley's first Sun Records single "That's All Right."

Randy Travis

I keep waiting for you to forgive me,
And you say that you can't even start,
And I feel like a stone
You have picked up and thrown,
To the hard rock bottom of your heart.

"Hard Rock Bottom of Your Heart"
Written by Hugh Prestwood
Recorded by Randy Travis

#2 Song of the Year in 1990

These rose-colored glasses
That I'm looking through,
Show only the beauty,
'Cause they hide all the truth;
And they let me hold onto the good times,
The good lines,
The ones I used to hear when I held you.

"Rose-Colored Glasses"
Written by John Conlee an George Baber
Recorded by John Conlee

$\mathcal{W}$ell, I never felt more like singing the blues,
'Cause I never thought that I'd ever lose
Your love, dear —
Why'd you do me this way?

"Singing the Blues"
Written by Melvin Endsley
Recorded by Marty Robbins

#10 Song of the Year for Marty Robbins in 1956 and went on the following year to be #11.

I didn't tell her each day I loved her;
I took it for granted somehow she knew.
I didn't hold her when she needed a shoulder;
It's not what I did,
It's what I didn't do.

"What I Didn't Do"
Written by Wood Newton and Michael Noble
Recorded by Steve Wariner

If teardrops were pennies
And heartaches were gold,
I'd have all the treasures
My pockets could hold.

"If Teardrops Were Pennies"
Written by Carl Butler
Recorded by Dolly Parton and Porter Wagoner

#25 Song of the Year in 1973

George Jones

If drinkin' don't kill me, her memory will.
I can't hold on much longer, the way I feel.
With the blood from my body,
I could start my own still.
If drinkin' don't kill me, her memory will.

"If Drinkin' Don't Kill Me"
Written by Harlan Sanders and Rick Beresford
Recorded by George Jones

John Anderson

I fell in the water that you walked on,
Up to my heart in misery;
Can't believe you're gone,
Thought you could do no wrong,
I fell in the water that you walked on.

"I Fell in the Water"
Written by Jeff Stevens and Jerry Salley
Recorded by John Anderson

Why don't you love me like you used to do?
How come you treat me like a worn-out shoe?
My hair is still curly and my eyes are still blue,
Why don't you love me like you used to do?

"Why Don't You Love Me"
Written by Hank Williams, Sr.
Recorded by Hank Williams, Sr.

#4 Song of the Year in 1950

Tricia Yearwood

I guess some things we bury
Are just bound to rise again,
For even if the whole world has forgotten,
The song remembers when.

"The Song Remembers When"
Written by Hugh Prestwood
Recorded by Tricia Yearwood

She brightened up the day
Like the early morning sun,
And she made what I was doing
Seem worthwhile.
It's the closest thing to living
That I guess I've ever known,
And it made me want to smile . . .
When I loved her.

"When I Loved Her"
Written by Kris Kristofferson
Recorded by Kris Kristofferson

Kris Kristofferson

*H*ear the whisper of the raindrops,
Blowing soft against the window,
And make believe you love me
   one more time,
For the good times.

"For the Good Times"
Written by Kris Kristofferson
Originally recorded by Ray Price, and later recorded by Kris Kristofferson.

Ray Price's recording was 1970's #2 Song of the Year and won a Grammy the same year for Best Male Country Vocal. Kris Kristofferson later recorded "For the Good Times" on his album *Me and Bobby McGee*.

Willie Nelson

*I*n the twilight glow I see her,
Blue eyes crying in the rain;
As we kissed goodbye and parted,
I knew we'd never meet again.

"Blue Eyes Crying in the Rain"
Written by Fred Rose
Recorded by Willie Nelson

Willie Nelson's recording was the 1975 #3 Song of the Year and later that year won the Grammy for Best Male Country Vocal.

*W*hy can't I forget you
And start my life anew,
Instead of having sweet dreams
About you?

"Sweet Dreams"
Written by Don Gibson
Recorded by Faron Young, Don Gibson and Patsy Cline

#13 Song of the Year in 1956 for Faron Young, #32 Song of the Year in 1961 for Don Gibson, and #23 Song of the Year in 1963 for Patsy Cline.

Pay Daze

Take this job and shove it,
I ain't workin' here no more.
My woman done left and took all the reasons
I was workin for.

"Take This Job and Shove It"
Written by David Allen Coe
Recorded by Johnny Paycheck

#6 Song of the Year in 1978

*Y*ou load sixteen tons, what do you get?
Another day older and deeper in debt.
Saint Peter, don't you call me
Cause I can't go;
I owe my soul
To the company store.

"Sixteen Tons"
Written by Merle Travis
Recorded by Tennessee Ernie Ford

#21 Song of the Year in 1955

Travis Tritt

*U*ncle Sam's got his hands in my pockets,
And he helps himself each time
   he needs a dime;
Them politicians treat me like a mushroom,
'Cause they feed me bull
and keep me in the blind.

"Lord Have Mercy on the Working Man"
Written by Kostas
Recorded by Travis Tritt

I got them steadily depressin',
Low down, mind messin',
Working at the car wash blues.

"Workin' at the Car Wash Blues"
Written by Jim Croce
Recorded by Jerry Reed

Fussin' and Cussin'

Hank Williams, Sr.

*W*hy do we stay together?
We always fuss and fight.
You ain't never known to be wrong,
And I ain't never been right.

"I Just Don't Like This Kind of Livin'"
Written by Hank Williams, Sr.
Recorded by Hank Williams, Sr.

$\mathcal{I}$'m overworked and I'm overweight;
I can't remember when I last had a date.
Oh, I didn't expect it to go down this way.

"Didn't Expect It to Go Down This Way"
Written by K. T. Oslin
Recorded by K. T. Oslin

*W*hy don't you mind your own business,
Mind your own business?
Well, if you mind your own business,
Then you won't be mindin' mine.

"Mind Your Own Business"
Written by Hank Williams, Sr.
Originally recorded by Hank Williams, Sr.,
and later recorded by Hank Williams, Jr.

#22 Song of the Year in 1987 for Hank Williams, Jr., nearly 40 years after it was written
and recorded by his father.

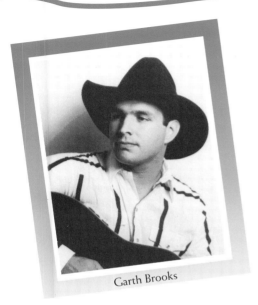

Garth Brooks

*A*ll my cards are on the table,
With no ace left in the hole,
And I'm much too young
To feel this damn old.

"Much Too Young (To Feel This Damn Old)"
Written by R. Taylor and Garth Brooks
Recorded by Garth Brooks

The #64 Song of the Year in 1989. "Much Too Young" was Garth Brooks' first single.

There's flies in the kitchen,
I can hear 'em there buzzin';
And I ain't done nothing
Since I woke up today.
How the hell can a person
Go to work in the morning,
And come home in the evening
And have nothing to say?

Bonnie Raitt

"Angel from Montgomery"
Written by John Prine
Recorded by John Prine and Bonnie Raitt

𝒴ou better stop telling lies about me,
Or I'm gonna tell the truth about you.

"You Better Stop Telling Lies About Me"
Written by Vaughn Horton
Recorded by Vaughn Horton

Tom T. Hall

*Y*ou have the nerve to tell me
You think that as a mother I'm not fit;
Well, this is just a little Peyton Place,
And you're all Harper Valley hypocrites.

"Harper Valley PTA"
Written by Tom T. Hall
Recorded by Jeanie C. Riley

#9 Song of the Year in 1968. That year Jeanie C. Riley's recording won both the Grammy for Best Female Country Vocal and the CMA "Song of the Year" award.

*I*f it wasn't for women,
What would you do?
Who would you tell
Your lies and troubles to?

"Leave Us Women Alone"
Written by Audrey Williams
Recorded by Audrey Williams

Hank Williams, Sr.'s wife Audrey was a performer and recording artist in her own right, frequently appearing with Hank on the Grand Ole Opry.

Buckaroos

Willie Nelson

*M*y heroes have always been cowboys,
And they still are it seems,
Sadly in search of, and one step in back of
Themselves and their slow-moving dreams.

"My Heroes Have Always Been Cowboys"
Written by Sharon Vaughn
Recorded by Willie Nelson

#13 Song of the Year in 1980

*O*h, carry me back to the lone prairie,
Where the coyotes howl, and the wind blows free;
When I die, you can bury me
'Neath the western skies, on the lone prairie.

"Carry Me Back to the Lone Prairie"
Written by Carson Robinson
Originally recorded by Eddy Arnold and later recorded by The Sons of The Pioneers.

*O*h give me land, lots of land,
Under starry skies above,
Don't fence me in.
Let me ride through the wide open country
That I love,
Don't fence me in.
Let me be by myself, in the evening breeze,
Listen to the murmur of the cottonwood trees,
Send me off forever, but I ask you please,
Don't fence me in.

"Don't Fence Me In"
Written by Cole Porter
Originally recorded by Roy Rogers and later recorded by both Bing Crosby
and The Andrews Sisters.

This song was featured in the Roy Rogers and Gabby Hayes movie of the same name.

*O*h, the wayward wind
Is a restless wind,
A restless wind that yearns to wander,
And I was born the next of kin,
The next of kin to the wayward wind.

"Wayward Wind"
Written by Herb Newman and Stan Lebowsky
Originally recorded by Gogi Grant. Also recorded by Tex Ritter.

Home Sweet Home

*A*ny old place I hang my hat
Is home sweet home to me.

"Brakeman's Blues"
Written by Jimmie Rodgers
Recorded by Jimmie Rodgers

Jimmie Rodgers was known as "The Singing Brakeman" in recognition of the 14 years he worked on the railroad. He was also called "The Father of Country Music," having record-ed the first country songs in Bristol, Tennessee, with RCA Victor's field recording execu-tive. Jimmie died from tuberculosis in a New York hotel room on May 26, 1933, following his last recording session. His body was returned home on a funeral train.

*O*h, we sure like to roam;
There's a ramblin' fever down in our bones.
Well, we're always home, but we're always gone,
Livin' in a mobile home.

"Livin' in a Mobile Home"
Written by Rory Michael Bourke and Ronny Scaife
Recorded by The Riders In The Sky

Thank God for kids —
There's magic for awhile,
A special kind of sunshine in a smile.
Do you ever stop to think or wonder why,
The nearest thing to heaven is a child?

"Thank God for Kids"
Written by Eddy Raven
Recorded by The Oak Ridge Boys

I'm seeing my father in me
I guess that's how it's meant to be
And I find I'm more and more like him each day
I notice I walk the way he walks
I notice I talk the way he talks
I'm startin' to see my father in me

"Seein' My Father In Me"
Written by Paul Overstreet
Recorded by Paul Overstreet

#16 Song of The Year in 1990

I'm a plain old country boy,
A cornbread lovin' country boy.
I raise Cain on Saturday,
But I go to church on Sunday;
I'm a plain old country boy.

"Country Boy"
Written by Felice Bryant and Boudleaux Bryant
Recorded by Jimmy Dickens

The Country Music Hall of Fame honors the husband and wife songwriting team of Felice and Boudleaux Bryant, whose work includes The Everly Brothers' hits "Bye, Bye Love" and "Wake Up, Little Susie."

Johnny Cash

$\mathcal{D}$ addy sang bass, Mama sang tenor,
Me and Little Brother would
   join right in there;
Singing seems to help the troubled soul.

"Daddy Sang Bass"
Written by Carl Perkins
Recorded by Johnny Cash

#2 Song of the Year in 1969

83

These highway 40 blues —
I've walked holes in both my shoes,
Counted the days since I've been gone,
And I'd love to see the lights of home.
Wasted time and money too,
Squandered youth in search of truth.

"Highway 40 Blues"
Written by Larry Cordle
Recorded by Ricky Skaggs

#29 Song of the Year in 1983

$\mathcal{D}$ addy, won't you take me back to Muhlenburg County,
Down by the Green River where paradise lay?
Well, I'm sorry, my son, but you're too late in asking;
Mister Peabody's coal train done hauled it away.

"Paradise"
Written by John Prine
Originally recorded by John Prine, later recorded by Lynn Anderson.

When it's late in the evening I climb up the hill,
And survey all my kingdom while everything's still.
Only me and the sky and an ol' whippoorwill,
Singin' songs in the twilight on mockin'bird hill.

"Mockin'bird Hill"
Written by Vaughn Horton
Recorded by Vaughn Horton

Bill Monroe

$\mathcal{L}$ate in the evening, about sundown,
High on the hill and above the town,
Uncle Penn played the fiddle —
Lord, how it would ring;
You could hear it talk,
You could hear it sing.

"Uncle Pen"
Written by Bill Monroe
Originally recorded by Bill Monroe and later recorded by Ricky Skaggs.

#20 Song of the Year in 1984 for Ricky Skaggs

I've searched this whole world over
Since I've been around;
I've never found a place
Like the old hometown.

"The Old Hometown"
Written by Lester Flatt
Recorded by Lester Flatt

Lost and Lonesome

Hank Williams, Sr.

I'm a rolling stone, all alone and lost;
For a life of sin, I have paid the cost.
When I pass by, all the people say,
"Just another guy on the lost highway."

"Lost Highway"
Written by Leon Payne
Recorded by Hank Williams, Sr.

Though he was best known for recording his own songs, Hank Williams, Sr., would make exceptions for songs he particularly liked. This song, by Capitol recording artist Leon Payne, was one of those exceptions.

*M*y pocketbook is empty,
And my heart is filled with pain;
I'm a thousand miles from home,
Just waiting for a train.

"Waiting For A Train"
Written by Jimmie Rodgers
Recorded by Jimmie Rodgers

Jimmie Rodgers recorded 56 songs in five years.

*H*ear that lonesome whippoorwill,
He sounds too blue to fly.
The midnight train is whining low,
I'm so lonesome I could cry.

"I'm So Lonesome I Could Cry"
Written by Hank Williams, Sr.
Recorded by Hank Williams, Sr.

*W*here to now, do you know?
One thing's for certain —
Gonna reap just what you sow;
And all you planted was heartache and pain —
Don't look now, but it looks like rain.

"Nowhere Bound"
Written by Monty Powell and Jule Medders
Recorded by Diamond Rio

#65 Song of the Year in 1992

*W*hen the time rolls around
For me to lay down and die,
I bet I'll have to go and hire me
Someone to cry.

"Nobody's Lonesome for Me"
Written by Hank Williams, Sr.
Recorded by Hank Williams, Sr.

*E*verybody's goin' out and havin' fun;
I'm just a fool for stayin' home and havin' none.
I can't get over how she set me free —
Oh, lonesome me.

"Oh, Lonesome Me"
Written by Don Gibson
Originally recorded by Don Gibson and later recorded by The Kentucky Headhunters.

#1 Song of the Year for Don Gibson in 1958 and #73 Song of the Year in 1990 for The Kentucky Headhunters.

*Y*ou know that old trees just grow stronger,
And old rivers grow wilder every day;
Old people just grow lonesome,
Waiting for someone to say,
"Hello in there,
Hello."

"Hello In There"
Written by John Prine
Recorded by John Prine

Honky - Tonkin'

No, we don't fit in with that white collar crowd,
We're a little too rowdy and a little too loud,
But there's no place that I'd rather be than right here,
With my red neck, white socks, and Blue Ribbon beer.

"Red Necks, White Socks, and Blue Ribbon Beer"
Written by Bob McDill, Wayland Holyfield and Chuck Neese
Recorded by Johnny Russell

#44 Song of the Year in 1973

*W*ell, there's one for the money,
Two for the show,
Three to get ready,
Now go, cat, go —
But don't you step on my blue suede shoes;
You can do anything,
But lay off of my blue suede shoes.

"Blue Suede Shoes"
Written by Carl Perkins
Recorded by Carl Perkins and also recorded by Elvis Presley.

#4 Song of the Year in 1956 for Carl Perkins on Sun Records.
This song was inspired by a chance remark Carl Perkins overheard on the dance floor
while working as a bandleader.

E verybody told me you can't get far
On thirty-seven dollars and a cheap guitar;
Now I'm smokin' into Texas with the hammer down,
And a rockin' little combo from the guitar town.

"Guitar Town"
Written by Steve Earle
Recorded by Steve Earle

*S*moke, smoke, smoke that cigarette;
Puff, puff, puff, and if you smoke yourself to death,
Tell St. Peter at the Golden Gate
That you hate to make him wait,
But you got to have another cigarette.

"Smoke, Smoke, Smoke"
Written by Merle Travis and Tex Williams
Originally recorded by Tex Williams and later recorded
by Dan Hicks and his Hot Licks.

#1 Song of the Year in 1947. Under pressure to come up with a song for a recording session, Tex Williams called on his friend Merle Travis and told him he needed a good song and fast. They lit up, started writing, and 20 minutes later had finished this song.

*I*t's almost dawn,
And the cops are gone —
Let's all get Dixie fried.

"Dixie Fried"
Written by Carl Perkins and Howard Griffin
Recorded by Carl Perkins

*H*e said, "I dance now at every chance and honky-tonk,
For drinks and tips,
But most the time is spent behind these county walls —
Hell, I drinks a bit."
He shook his head, and as he shook his head,
I heard someone ask him, "Please,
Mr. Bojangles,
Mr. Bojangles,
Mr. Bojangles,
Dance."

"Mr. Bojangles"
Written by Jerry Jeff Walker
Originally recorded by Jerry Jeff Walker and later recorded
by The Nitty Gritty Dirt Band.

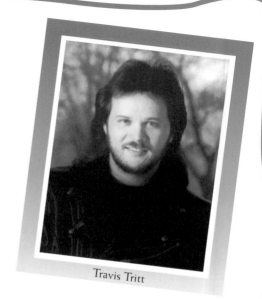

Travis Tritt

I need one good honky-tonk angel
To turn my life around —
That's reason enough for me to lay
This ol' bottle down.
A woman warm and willin',
That's what I'm looking for,
'Cause the whiskey ain't workin' anymore.

"The Whiskey Ain't Workin'"
Written by Ronny Scaife and Marty Stuart
Recorded by Travis Tritt and Marty Stuart

#55 Song of the Year in 1992.

Sweet Jesus

*O*ne day at a time, sweet Jesus,
That's all I'm asking of you.
Just give me the strength to do every day,
What I have to do.
Yesterday's gone, sweet Jesus,
And tomorrow may never be mine —
Lord help me today, show me the way,
One day at a time.

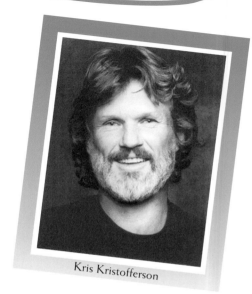

Kris Kristofferson

"One Day at a Time"
Written by Marijohn Wilkin and Kris Kristofferson
Recorded by Christy Lane

#2 Song of the Year in 1980

Blow up your TV,
Throw away your papers,
Move to the country,
Build you a home;
Plant a little garden,
Eat a lot of peaches,
Try to find Jesus
On your own.

"Spanish Pipe Dream"
Written by John Prine
Recorded by John Prine

Hank Williams, Sr.

I saw the light, I saw the light,
No more darkness, no more night.
Now I'm so happy, no sorrow in sight,
Praise the Lord! I saw the light.

"I Saw the Light"
Written by Hank Williams, Sr.
Recorded by Hank Williams, Sr.

In just six years Hank Williams wrote approximately 125 songs.

*J*esus and Mama always loved me,
Even when the Devil took control;
Jesus and Mama always loved me —
This I know.

"Jesus and Mama"
Written by Danny Bear Mayo and James Dean Hicks
Recorded by Confederate Railroad

*W*hen troubles surround us, when evils come,
The body grows weak, the spirit grows numb;
When these things beset us, He doesn't forget us —
He sends down His love, on the wings of a dove.

"Wings of a Dove"
Written by Bob Ferguson
Originally recorded by Ferlin Husky and later recorded by Porter Wagoner.

#10 Song of the Year for Ferlin Husky in both 1960 and 1961.
Sometimes I thank God

Garth Brooks

For unanswered prayers
 Remember when you're talking
 To the man upstairs
 Just because he may not answer
 Doesn't mean he don't care
 Some of God's greatest gifts
 Are unanswered prayers

"Unanswered Prayers"
Written by Pat Alger, Garth Brooks and Larry Bastain
Recorded by Garth Brooks

#9 Song of The Year in 1991

Copyright Information
Listed Alphabetically by Song Title

"(I'd Be) A Legend In My Time" written by Don Gibson
Copyright (c) 1960, Renewed 1988
Acuff-Rose Music, Inc.
International Rights Secured.
All Rights Reserved.

"A Pair Of Old Sneakers" by Larry Kingston, Glenn Sutton
Copyright (c) 1980, Songs of Polygram International, Inc.
& Peermusic, Ltd.
All Rights Reserved. Used by Permission.

"Ain't Necessarily So" by Beth Nielsen Chapman
Copyright (c) 1990, Warneractive Songs, Inc. (ASCAP) and
Macy Place Music (ASCAP c/o Warneractive Songs, Inc.)
All Rights Reserved. Made in USA.
Used by Permission of Warner Bros. Publications, Inc.,
Miami, FL 33014

"Smiles Are Made Out of Sunshine" by Ray Gilbert
Copyright (c) 1943 by Peer International Corporation
Copyright Renewed.
International Copyright Secured.
All Rights Reserved. Used by Permission.

"Smoke Smoke Smoke That Cigarette" by Merle Travis, Tex Williams
Copyright (c) 1947 (Renewed) Unichappell Music, Inc. (BMI) &
Elvis Presley Music (BMI)
All Rights on behalf of Elvis Presley Music administered by
Unichappell Music, Inc.
All Rights reserved. Made in USA.
Used by Permission of Warner Bros. Publications, Inc.,
Miami, FL 33014

"Someday Soon" by Ian Tyson
Copyright (c) 1991 Warner Bros., Inc. (ASCAP)
All Rights Reserved. Made in USA.
Used by Permission of Warner Bros. Publications, Inc., Miami, FL 33014

"Somewhere Between Ragged and Right" by Roger Murrah & Waylon Jennings.
Copyright (c) 1987 Tom Collins Music Corporation (BMI) and Waylon Jennings Music
(BMI). All rights administered by Irving Music on behalf of Waylon Jennings
Music for the world.
All Rights Reserved. Used by Permission.